My Heart Is Yours

Christine J. Logan

My Heart is Yours
ISBN 978-0-9869229-2-3

Other books by Christine Logan

To Touch Your Heart
ISBN 978-0-9869229-0-0

Special Tribute to Mothers Everywhere
co-written with Gordon Baird
ISBN 978-0-9869229-1-6

Author and Cover Art by Christine Logan
Poems also in Maple Ridge Festival of Light (2011)
And Famous Poets of the Heartland (2007).

Contents

I dedicate this book in honor of the memory
of my little brother.

Riccy Charles Mackay
(July 18, 1972 - August 28, 2010)
We love you and miss you!

xoxo

Acknowledgements

My biggest thanks goes to God. Thank You for giving me the courage, love and patience to endure whatever comes.

I wish to thank all of Riccy's friends (and our family) for their amazing love of my brother. God rest his soul.

My heart goes out to everyone with sincere thanks for helping and supporting me in every aspect of this journey of becoming a published author and a hopeful support in causes to help others.

A special thanks to Rick Vandenberg and Melanie Iddon at Infinite Gravity Digital Media (www.infinitegravity.com), for their kindness in helping me with my web design.

And thank you to my beautiful hand model, Lauren Brunton

My url is (www.cloganinsideinspiration.com)

RICCY

There is no other who would lack
To help you out and watch your back

Ric's love sincere, his friends so dear
His family there in a pinch

You may think life is hard
But to Riccy, it's just a cinch

Keep in mind, focus on the good
Never lose sight
His intensions were never misunderstood

Love is what counts
Family and friends

His memory in our hearts
Never ends.

FAMILY TREE

Inside this family heart
Lives a family tree
Strong, loving vines from the start
With thorns of hate weeded out

Strength of love was born in me
With painful slivers along the way
Love overcame and washed them away

Family roots grow very deep
With memories and love
Meant for sharing, not ours to keep

Like grains of sand
That passes through time
Stories are handed on down the line

With all that's said and done with this
A family tree is God's great gift.

THANKS TO YOU

Since a child, born Christmas day
Family and friends would guide my way

Through trials and tragedies,
Hard work and doubt
With family and friends by my side
My faith never runs out

An adult now, full of hope
There isn't anything I cannot cope

With a heart full of love and caring
Everything I am is blessed with sharing.

VALUE YOUR LIFE

Value your life
It's not your own
Walking carelessly
Leaves loved ones alone

Alone, you have left us
Your head filled with distractions
Your feet were too careless
Reckless, your actions

Your actions, we try not to blame
Or hold any anger
To dishonor your name

Our hearts filled with sorrow
Our minds trapped in the past
We live on without you
With our memories that holdfast.

THINKING OF YOU

From the first light of day
To the end of the night
Each passing moment
Your love is in sight

Blessings be with You
Happiness too
Your love guides me
To be close to You.

STEPS WE TAKE

Each step we take, unlike another
His love for us is like no other

Each step forward, never back
If we receive His love
His strength in us would never lack

Each step unknown
Take them with grace
For others we meet, with hopes we pray
That one day, they too
Will come face to face
With our Father in Heaven

We're never alone
With each step we take.

GENTLE WIND

Gentle wind, how you caress the leaves
In the trees with your grace and tenderness
Each leaf dancing with joy
As you play around them

Gentle wind, how you delicately hold a bird in
flight
Each bird holding onto your embrace
With pure delight

Gentle wind, your purpose only to put
Things in their place
While putting smiles on every face

Gentle wind, soft, gentle wind.

HOME FOR ME

Home for me
A memory in my past
A friendship that never ends
A love that always lasts

Home for me
Is where I lay my head
Could be while I travel,
Visit my mom at her house
Or at home in my very own bed

Home is not taken for granted
It's how you feel inside
It's a goal we should carry with us
It's a blessing without pride

Home for me is Heaven bound
With Jesus by my side
Learn from Him
Follow your heart
Truth will set you free
Home, you then will find.

BECAUSE OF HIM

It's not what we accomplish
That gets us through the day
It's the strength of the Lord within us
That carries us His way

His spirit is alive
If only we believe
That He is God's
Alive and well
It's up to us
To share and tell

Tell others He is good news
He'll walk you through your troubles
Turn away and don't believe
And all your worries double

It's not our choice
We must be humble

We must forgive and love and trust
Then all your sins, if you are sorry
Are certainly forgiven
They will definitely crumble

It's only with His grace
His forgiveness and His love
That one day we will be chosen
We will be among His love.

MY HEART IS YOURS

My heart is Yours
So You may know
How much my love for You has grown

My heart has never been my own
It's always searching for love unknown

Unknown to others
Until they see
The joy and peace and grace
You bring in me

My heart is worn upon my sleeve
For all the people I meet to see
So they may see the light I carry
My peace, my joy, it's never scary

My heart tells me
My hope in You, is so that others
May find You too
And believe.

I'LL STAND

I'll stand by You
Stand up for You
Stand hand in hand
And die for You

My love for You is growing stronger
I'm never alone
I'm not lonely any longer
By myself, I'm not alone
My life is Yours
I know where I'm goin'

I'm goin' to go wherever You want me
I'm goin' to stand strong
No one can taunt me

I'm standing for love
I'm standing for truth
I'm standing for Jesus
I'm standing for You.

Christine J. Logan

PRETTY IS A LITTLE GIRL

Pretty is a little girl
New dress on, anxious to twirl
Roses on her cheeks
Kisses on her brow
Music starts, brother cries
Sister says, "oh Nicky, not now!"
Mother is their comfort
Full of love and praise
Brother stops his crying
Sister takes a bow
Happiness fills their days
Father's home, day's complete
Kids tucked in bed, nice and neat
Kiss for mom," I love you", then said
Praise the Lord, let's go to bed.

PATTY'S PILLOW

Patricia took a piece of me
She put it beneath her pillow

She praises, she cares
She sees in me
The silly I keep so deep
As deep as the roots of a weeping willow tree

She holds me dear
As close as her pillow
I know that may sound crazy
But to me, she's as sweet as a daisy

Patricia is Patty, she's my best friend
With all she has, it's clear to many
She's a wonderful friend
With her hand held open
For all to lend

Once you get to know her
Don't ever let her go
She has an abundant amount of love to share
I'm blessed to be her friend

So put my love beneath your pillow
you'll awaken to find and know it's real
when love and friendship have no limits
you'll know your heart is always in it.

Christine J. Logan

MY BEST FRIEND

(Written by Patty Poirier)

My best friend's name is Christine
She stands above the rest

When I'm down, she's always around
With the heart of an angel
She's always there with a kind word

She cares about everybody
With a smile that can brighten any room

She is as silly as she can be
Her heart is pure, pure as can be

Her faith in God is immense

When we are together
There is no place I'd rather be
Than with my best friend, Christine

FACTS AND TRUTH

Facts and truth are history
Tomorrow's day a mystery

Stories told of times now gone
our minds can't fathom from beyond
beyond our sight, out of reach
What we know, is what we teach

If we acknowledge what we conceive
there's nothing in the world
We can't achieve

Be a good person, do no wrong
Try your best and it won't be long

It won't be long, before you know
Your heart will change
Only love will show.

SHIMMER

Shimmer is the sun
On the ripples of a lake
The stars in the sky
And icing on a cake

Shimmer is the shine within
A diamond on your finger
The gentle drip from an icicle in winter

Shimmer is a blanket of snow
With sun shining over the meadow
Over the meadow, the glistening sparkle
Covers completely, how remarkable!

Shimmers are a simple pleasure
In our hearts, we should always treasure.

JESUS KNOCKED

Jesus knocked upon my door
For years, I turned Him away

He knocked again
I learned to know
His love was here to stay

So when He knocked, I let Him in
With my arms open wide

No one said, "I must!"
No one said, " I better!"
I realized, there is no love greater

I learned about the truth
I learned about His love
I received these blessings
I have been given
Because of our Father above.

YOU HAVE NO IDEA

You have no idea, when you're not there
How much I see you everywhere

For all that you are
You've come so far
Since a funny, little ham
To a strong, independent woman

You bring me joy, in just the thought of you
Without my memories, I would surely come
unglued

Thank you, Mary, for who you are
Have faith in yourself
And you will go far

Forgive always, overcome your doubts
And always look ahead
Giving your love is more powerful
Than making "the bread"

So, keep in mind, when you have no idea
Of how much you're loved, you'll know
Your mama sees you everywhere
With heart and love and soul.

IMAGINE

Imagine days
with sunshine and rainbows

Imagine nights
That expands through the sky

Imagine the ocean
Mysterious and deep

Imagine miracles that happen
With no questions of why

Easy to do, it's true

But I could never imagine
My life without you.

BACK IN THE DAY

Push on a swing
Game of crib
Frisbee spinning in the wind
Step over the cracks
Don't break mother's back
Show called, "Land of the Lost"

Treasure of coins baked in your cake
Bracelet filled with charms
Back then, was quite a cost

Baby tooth beneath your pillow
Game of "Hide and Seek"
Counting underneath a weeping willow
Remember not to peek

Making forts, running through trails
Treasures of the past
Experience them all over again
Make the memories last.

STRIVE WHAT YOU'VE GOT

I don't strive for the best
But I strive what I've got
It isn't a little, it isn't a lot
It's enough for me, for you to see
What life's simple pleasures can bring
This should be our most treasured things
Strive to give and help a friend
The Lord will take care of us
In the end.

THUNDER AND LIGHTNING

Thunder and lightning, my oh my
How your fury and beauty ignite the sky

Your power majestic
Your timing quite rare
Many have tried to take on your dare

One wrong timing, in the wrong place
Can put the strongest of man
Flat on his face

Be it excitement or fear
Let us cheer, praise and shout
Cheer for your beauty
Praise, for which you belong
Shout for the Lord
He created it all

Thunder and lightning
Best admired from inside looking out
It's safer this way
Without any doubt.

BECAUSE OF YOU

Because You care, You're always there
Because You love me, my sins You spare
Because I ask, You fill my heart
With Your Holy Spirit
For my day to start

Because my faith in You is strong
You bless me in knowing
To stay away from wrong

Because I can, because it's Your will
You lead me to others, with their hearts to fill

Fill them with faith, truth and love
And guide them with purpose
To receive Your love.

TELL YOUR FRIENDS

I recommend you tell your friends
How much they mean to you
How much you care
One day you're looking for them
And they're no longer there
Tell them you'll cherish them always
Cherish them in your heart
For certainty comes
Leaving you far apart
Far apart in flesh
But not in our souls
Love everyone
Make it part of your goals
We miss you now and love you still
Thank God for friendship
It is His will.

FREE SPIRIT

Feel the breeze upon your face
In the night or start of day
To ride carefree and in the wind
At any given time
Fills you with a burst of life
You'll gladly spend the dime
Ride with your friends
Or on your own
Ride for a cause
Let your heart be shown
Go ride but be safe
Leave the world behind
And focus ahead
Your journey is long
So, set your spirit free

LITTLE BUDS

Twelve little buds
Ready to bloom
Gather in a corner
Of my little room
All twelve buds
Open in sync
Looking for the light
Turning to pink
Amazing and proud
They all stand tall
With water and love
They will not fall
Twelve little buds
Close up tight
Almost dark now
Ready for the night.

WHAT'S MINE IS YOURS

Take my hand
Take my love
Just don't take me for granted

Take my clothes
Take my car
I don't have much
You won't get far

Take my heart
Take my well wishes
Take my laugh with you
It will keep you in stitches

Take my light
Take my sight
Take my time
Just don't take what isn't mine.

CHERISH HIS CREATIONS

Big city lights can never compare
To the beauty and gaze
From a forest lake's stare
Imagine the ripples from one tiny pebble
A stone throw away
From the big city rebel
Wild flowers and cat's tails
Surrounded by beauty and light
From the stars in the sky
That dance through the night
Walk from the city
To the wilderness so pretty
Cherish the lush, green scene
Walking through trails where you've never been
Nature's creations were made with love
From our Father in heaven
Our Lord up above.

ADORE ME NOT

Adore me not, for I am small
Courageous and humble
Before you all

To live as He, I try my best
To give my all before I rest

Allow my heart, my gift to you
To light the way
And follow through

The trail is tight with thorns and darkness
I overcome with the power of happiness

Happiness, truth and light
Will set you free
From what's not right

Do not adore those of the flesh
But He, Himself and His holiness.

Christine J. Logan

FIND YOUR PLACE

Find a place where you belong
It will feel right, you will be strong
You will have courage
To be who you are
You'll feel peace inside
And shimmer like a star
Shining on others
So your light from within you
Will brighten sad days
When others feel blue
You will belong from where you are meant
To your purpose on earth
So make it time well spent
Spend it on others
Your time and your love
And you will find glory
In your home up above.

SPECIAL DAY

(Dedicated to Kieran)

This day is special
This day is yours
From the birth of your great grandma
To the western shores
Western shores
Where mystical winds blow
We're anxiously waiting
For your precious face to show

Show us your light
Show us your love
From this day onward
Our love for you is endless
Like the stars above.

ISN'T IT FUNNY

Isn't it funny
When you're down on your luck
How faith lifts you up
Like lightning has struck

Isn't it funny
When depression sets in
How it's taken from you
Within moments, from Him

Isn't it funny
When you ask, you receive
It's all in the timing
With His love, He graciously gives
When we believe

Isn't it funny
When we are stubborn, we fall
When His love is there for us
We have no idea at all

Isn't it funny
How it takes just a second
To ask in our hearts
To forgive us and bless us
How much He wants this
To favor His love
And let us all know, there IS peace from above.

Christine J. Logan

BLESS US ALL

Bless us all, so we may know
How much love You have to show

Un-ending love
With a price already paid
Thanks to Your Son
In my heart, Jesus lay

Jesus forgave my sins
Because I asked
For tomorrow, today
And sins from my past

He fills up my heart
To be as good as His
I try my best
to honor Him with this

Because He forgives me
And love fills my heart
My relationship with God
Is ready to start

Thank You, Lord
For loving me

I pray this love for others
So they may see and find
Nothing on earth compares
Like your love for me
For us
A love with the strongest bind.

TREASURES

A treasure is so
In the eye of the beholder
It does not change
Because we get older

A tiny piece of paper
With the words, "I love you, "written down
To some, is worth more
Than a golden crown

From a stuffed teddy bear or a favorite hat
Or even a worn out T shirt
All have been comfort to some kind of hurt

A treasure, sometimes, is hard to give up
Especially when you're down on your luck

But sharing your treasure
With a stranger or more
Will make you feel better
And keep your heart pure.

SAVE ME FROM MYSELF

Save me from myself
Save me from my sins
Satan's trying to get a hold on me
Looking for easy ways to get in

He's sneaky and intrusive
Always trying to catch me off guard
He works his way into my dreams
Where I really have no control

But, when I wake, I realize
It's creative and slick in this mind of mine
Therefore, he can never take hold

So, thank You, Lord, for saving me
When awake and when I sleep
This evil one can try all he wants
But he'll never again
Get more than a peek.

WHEN YOU'RE WALKING

When you're walking
Your feet are talking
A breath with every step

When you're smiling
You're reconciling
Your heart with those you've met
When you're giving
You're really living
Free from guilt and fret

When you're at peace in your heart
Every day, a love - filled start
Will come without regret

Choose your path
Peace or wrath
And your future will be set.

STEPPING STONES

Gently stepping on the stones of life
With tippy toes and care
Different paths for each of us
Mine, to be a wife

The path I've chosen in the past
Led me to who I am today
A mom, a friend, a sister too
Regrets forgiven so not to last

I pray our paths be pairing
Hoping they lead to the same place
Across that last stone, into heaven
Where our Father's love
We'll be sharing.

SEEING IS A BLESSING

I see Him in my heart
I see Him in my mind
His love for me is precious and kind

I see myself with you
I see myself with Him
With this much love inside me
My light will never go dim

I see you struggle
I see your worries and heartache
All can be eased
With each step you take

A step of faith
A step of hope
Will lead you to truth
And help you cope.

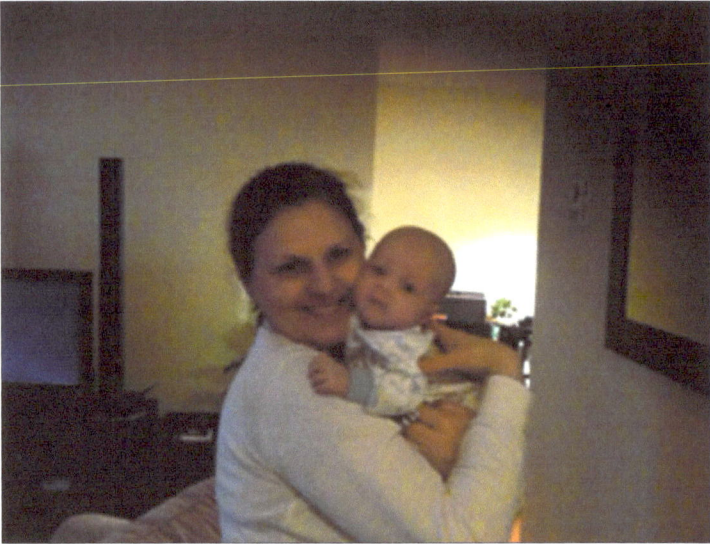

LOGAN

(Dedicated to Logan)

This Logan I speak of, is not my name
It's not the lake or city they claim

This Logan you're about to learn of
Is sweet and precious
And newly heard of

He's a beautiful boy
Born not long ago
With a family that loves him
And are anxious to show

This Logan has a purpose
He's meant to be here
He was blessed with life
Followed by a tear

Those tears of joy
Made him whole
God's grace and His love
Played a huge role.

NEVER HUNGRY

This is a day that starts from new
How you look at it, is up to you

From the minute you wake
From your warm, sleepy bed
Ask for His love
And you will be spiritually fed

This kind of food never diminishes
Share it with others
Until your day finishes

The second you ask, you will receive
Your only task is that you believe

Each day the same
But a little bit different
His love for you never changes
It's always magnificent

So, each day you wake
From your warm, sleepy bed
Ask to be filled with His love
And be fed.

FRAGILE

My shell is fragile
I'm an open book
You don't have to break me
To get a good look

I'm easy to read
And easily pleased
My heart tells my hands
Keep in clear view
Where they may be needed
When it is my cue

My shell is renewed
When my heart gets re-filled
With His spirit inside me
I'm instantly thrilled

God bless this joy
I carry inside
May my words never run out
As He stay by my side.

IN HONOR OF HIM

In honor of Him
I pray for you
You've been through a lot
You've been far from home
Your journey is over
But you're never alone
He waits for you
To give to you
His eternal love and grace
You had His Holy Spirit here
Now you live among Him
In His presence with no fear
With my love
And honor of Him
Take my prayers with you
And be free from all sin.

ALWAYS WITH ME

Do you ever feel like someone's watching you?
You look to the left
You look to the right
You look to the sky
You know He's close
And you know He's outa' sight!
I trust and know You're here to stay
It feels so right and I'm thankful every day
My heart is beating to a distant drum
It carries me through
Until the day You come
I once was lost and lonely
When I was alone
You came into my life
And filled me with peace and hope
Now when I'm alone, I'm never alone
I trust You Lord and thank You every day
For coming into my life
Where I know You're here to stay.

STILL HERE TODAY

I'm still here today
Going through the hours
As rainbows shine through the clouds

I'm still here today
Tallying up the minutes
Looking for roses to smell
Anxious to share my smile

I'm still here today
Seconds come at me again
I'll find them a home
Where love dwells within

I'm here today, His will to stay
Among my life, to share with yours
Tomorrow's day will come and go
My job on this earth
Will not let me go.

THE BEST READ ME

My bones grow older, tired and weak
Even my brain needs a major tweak
I may forget things, I may even sleep longer
But trust in me, my heart is getting stronger

My body is but an aging shell
With years gone by and stories to tell
I'm a walking, talking open book
Growing older with every look

What some people miss
What some don't see
Is the amount of love I can give
And the Spirit of Jesus burning in me

This is known to those who read between the lines
A love like this has the strongest bind

You may see and aging book
As you see me walking
Wait….. Then take another look

You see my heart, the love inside me
It shines for you

Let this love guide you
And seek the way
To shine on others
As our hearts never fade.

FOR YOU

To you who fought and survived the war
We honor you with heart and soul
You gave it your all
To save our land
The least we can do
Is hold your hand
We hold your hand and pray for you
Because our Father wants us to
Our Father is waiting to share His glory
With you and others who share a
Similar story
Your story is heard
Our hearts are grateful
For all you've done
We love you, we're thankful.

LAST WORDS

With love, they are given
Last words and a tear
One heart to another
From those we love, with no fear

With thanks, we can learn
Departures such as this
To forgive and move on
No regrets, but a kiss

With hope, for reunion
In heaven or on earth
To unite once again
Comes inevitable rebirth

With love and recognition
Last words will remain
In our hearts everlasting
Until we meet again.

Some Of My Favorite Quotes

"Love is patient, love is kind. It does not envy, it does not boast, it is not proud."

1 Corinthians 13:4 (the bible)

"If you're not living life on the edge, you're taking up too much room."

Unknown

"There is no cost in a kind word."

Unknown

"If you want what you've never had before, you've got to do what you've never done before."

My Aunty Nikki

"Allow your inspiration to spread to others."

Christine Logan

"If you don't believe in miracles, you're not a realist."

Unknown

And finally….. "Treat others, as you would have them treat you."

www.ingramcontent.com/pod-product-compliance
Lightning Source LLC
Chambersburg PA
CBHW042005100426
42736CB00037B/10